Creating International Christian Communities

Integrating Models of Urban Mission

Simon Cartwright
St Thomas' Community Minister,
Walbrook Epiphany Team and Assistant
Area Dean, Derby City

GROVE BOOKS LIMITED
RIDLEY HALL RD CAMBRIDGE CB3 9HU

Contents

Church Mission Society supports the Grove Mission and Evangelism Series
At Church Mission Society, we believe that every Christian is called to join in God's mission, whether that means crossing the street or crossing continents, and we want to set people free to put that call into action.

First Impression February 2020
ISSN 2399-6536
ISBN 978 1 78827 113 4

1 Introduction

The shape of mission and ministry is changing rapidly. In the Church of England, we have seen a number of new initiatives including fresh expressions, resource churches and new diocesan strategies to help us grow younger and transform traditional structures like deaneries and parishes into new drivers for mission.

At the same time, many commentators are suggesting that the future of the church may lie in an emphasis on small groups, with cathedrals or minster churches replacing the parish system.[1] These are certainly the two areas of growth I have observed in the church today. The latter is in gathered congregations offering one strand of Christianity in a well-funded and professionally led manner. The former is in the emergence of small Christian communities that take discipleship seriously and are seeking a highly contextual model of mission. By contrast, the churches that seem to be struggling are the traditional churches, led by a single member of the clergy, with an increasingly elderly laity sitting in pews on a Sunday.

The churches that seem to be struggling are the traditional churches

My own call to ordination came from a call to live and work in the inner city. It is within these multicultural and often deprived communities that we have seen some of the most intensive changes in the church, as traditional church congregations have dwindled and church buildings have closed. Ministering in such parishes has meant I have had to spend a lot of time in prayer and reflection on new and different models of urban mission. These have included: the combining of mission and pastoral care in lay chaplaincy; the transformative ideas of asset-based community development; and the prayerful entrepreneurialism of pioneer ministry.

On reflection, I see that the times of change and innovation we are witnessing are not unique to the twenty-first century. We have seen many periods in church history when the established church became dominated by a national and clerical agenda and lost its connection, particularly with the poor and needy. I believe we can trace a similar pattern in the Jews' story of exilic and post-exilic Israel as national, temple-based worship crumbled and the new synagogues emerged. In a similar manner, God seems to do a new thing in his church: from the Desert Fathers and the rise of monastic communities, to the

Reformation and the rise of free churches. Could the new forms of church that have emerged in recent years be another period when God is calling us to a new thing, and a return to radical forms of intentional Christian community?

This booklet begins with my own story and how this has shaped my experience of urban mission and ministry. I then analyze the models of urban mission that I have seen emerge, looking at how other churches have developed similar innovative ideas in chaplaincy, community development and pioneering. I then further reflect on these models through the lens of the Jewish story of faithful change during the exilic period. In so doing, I suggest that we need to integrate these models of urban mission in small, intentional Christian communities. Finally, I return to my own story and how I have sought to create such an intentional community, with a rhythm of life that draws on the ideas of new monasticism, in the St Thomas' Community in Derby.

2

My Story

'Where have all the Christians gone?' These challenging words echoed around the Spring Harvest venue, as pictures of inner-city deprivation were flashed on the screen. The year was 1987, about a year after the furore caused by the publication of the *Faith in the City* report.[2] It was a time of flux, when the church and government were thrown on the defensive over their lack of investment and commitment to inner-city areas.

Yet the challenge in that Spring Harvest venue went further. To the accompaniment of Graham Kendrick's song, 'God put the fighter in me,' the question that echoed in my ears was, 'Where have all the Christian soldiers gone?' It was a personal call. 'Will you take up the challenge and live and work in the inner city? Will you take a stand against injustice and seek God's kingdom in these forgotten parts of God's mission field?' I sat upright; I knew God was speaking to me, and so began my call to urban mission.

London

It began with a year out working for the church in south-east London. Then I trained to be a town planner and followed a career in urban regeneration: working in urban policy; project management; and facilitating community development. At the same time I lived in inner-city areas, and attended local churches, where together we sought to shine a light in dark places. I guess it was only a matter of time before I felt God's call to lead his church in the inner city.

Birmingham

My curacy was in Ward End, in inner East Birmingham. Supported by my training incumbent, who was based at the parish church down the road, I was based in the former parish of St Margaret's Ward End. This is a multi-ethnic parish (about 50% Pakistani Muslim) where the church building had recently closed. My role was to 'develop renewed pastoral contact in the area, to do most of the occasional offices in that area, develop relations with the school and community groups (with help from the church's community development worker); then in time to run *Alpha* courses, establish a cell group and help replant church in the area.'[3]

I began to make links with this multicultural community, working in partnership with the church's community development worker. This was mainly seen in the Overpool Working Group, a multi-agency partnership that included the local school, Sure Start, police, council officer and, most importantly, the local after-school club. While relationships were growing between the church's community development worker and the Muslim after-school club manager, I developed a particularly good rapport with the local council officer whom I will call *Jack*. He was one of those people Jesus calls 'a man of peace' for whenever we met there was a sense of peace (Luke 10.6). *Jack* would laughingly call me his chaplain and he began to share his problems with me. I listened and offered gentle pastoral care.

Then one day I woke up to blue flashing lights all down the street and TV cameras camped on the playing field. A counter-terrorism raid was underway and a number of local Asian young men were taken away for questioning. The undercurrents of community tensions began to grow rapidly. It was then that the relationship between the church's community development worker and the Muslim after-school club manager really came to the fore. We began to run a number of *ad hoc* events under the banner 'Creating Unity in the Community' including a community food festival, joint Christmas-Eid celebration and trips to the seaside.

We began work to reopen the closed church building as a community hub

It became clear to me that to sustain this unity, we needed more than one-off events; we needed to put the heart back into the community; and so we began work to reopen the closed church building as a community hub. The Overpool Working Group was reconstituted as a community development trust and we raised the money to reopen the church. But we needed someone to help us run the trust. I called *Jack*.

A year or so later, *Jack* had become the treasurer and was very active in our work. He commented to me, 'Why is it that when I work with you, I feel energized and yet my work in the council drains me?' I replied that it could be something to be do with God and left it at that. But a few months later, *Jack* agreed to join our *Alpha* Course. When I asked him what made him want to know more about the Christian faith, he said that it was by working alongside us, that he realized we had something he did not and he wanted to know what this peace was all about.

No church had been planted by the time I finished my curacy. The church rebuilding project had only just begun, but the work continued. Ten years later the church has reopened with a unity hub at its core, all based in the old church—interestingly managed by the former after-school club manager, with a new café church meeting on a Sunday afternoon.

Derby

In the meantime, I had moved to Derby to take up the post as a community minister working across four parishes in the inner city. This new role was to 'identify areas where the team ministry could work in cooperation and partnership with others to bless and serve the people of Normanton and to mobilize the churches and organize their resources (including buildings) in response to these opportunities.'[4]

Pear Tree, Normanton and Rose Hill are particularly disadvantaged areas. The relatively poor-quality terraced housing is occupied by migrant groups who first settle in the area before they raise sufficient income to move out. This leads to a very transient population—in the 2011 census, 22% of the population had been here less than 10 years, and since the census there has been a noticeable increase in people from the Middle East (Iraqi, Iranian and Kurdish) and East Africa (Eritrean, Sudanese and Somali.)

In the centre of this community lies St Thomas, a decaying Victorian church building that had already been listed on the English Heritage at-risk register, placing responsibility on us as owners to make urgent repairs. Yet the church was in a prime location opposite the library, next door to the health centre, across from the police station. We could not have chosen a better location for the community to know where the church was.

Closing St Thomas' felt like saying, 'The Anglican church has given up on you'

Sadly, the congregation was struggling due to old age and ill health, and it was decided that we merge all our worship at the main parish church—St Augustine's. However, I struggled with this; closing St Thomas' felt like putting a sign on the door saying, 'The Anglican church has given up on you.' So, once again, I was faced with the challenge of refurbishing a church building and reconnecting with the community at large.

I began to follow the twin approach developed in Ward End, a mixture of getting to know people by walking the streets offering gentle pastoral care to the people in the area in a ministry akin to chaplaincy, combined with building partnerships around community development projects, beginning with a food distribution project—working alongside FareShare, a charity who distribute unused food from the food industry to local charities that feed the hungry. The dusty church was cleaned and opened up once a fortnight to receive food for the food distribution projects in Derby.

Out of this project, a small group began to gather at St Thomas' for a weekly prayer meeting. It was a small beginning for a big vision to reopen St Thomas. The group became the core of a missional community committed to prayer, mission and hospitality. We fundraised to restore the building, and worship has been restored to the building on a regular basis.

But it was not just a building project. In the words of Cathy Ross from CMS, 'Relationship building must come first, and church will follow.'[5]

We are looking into ways we can use food and hospitality to enable the church to meet with the community. It is all about establishing a partnership so that the individuals and the organizations in our area are not just ministered to but empowered to change the Pear Tree, Normanton and Rose Hill area.

Just as happened in Ward End, we are seeing a church being restored and reopened as a centre for the local community, a community development-led approach, where my role is more akin to a chaplain. However, we have seen a congregation emerge earlier than in Ward End. I unexpectedly found myself as a pioneer, as the missional community is now established as the St Thomas' Community, complementing the main parish church in urban mission.

3

The Church's Story

My story reflects a trend in the Church of England as we have moved away from people attending church out of a sense of duty, towards greater emphasis on mission. Reviewing my story, I see three models of urban mission emerge: chaplaincy; community development; and pioneering fresh expressions of church. All these approaches are changing both how we put our faith into action and the roles of church leaders.

In this chapter, I want to analyze each of these three models of urban mission and see what they offer to the church today. To help illustrate these reflections, I have also included some case studies from projects in Derby that have inspired me on my journey.

A Church that Promotes Well-being—The Role of the Chaplain

In the previous chapter, I told *Jack's* story and recalled how we worked together for peace and well-being in our neighbourhood. It was interesting that *Jack* chose to call me his chaplain. This may be because chaplaincy is easier to understand in the secular world, especially when the idea of priests has been challenged in light of the child abuse scandals.

I find myself attracted to the idea of chaplaincy, especially as they work on the edge of faith communities. Unlike church-based ministries their primary focus is on working with other people who work in other areas in the life of society. A General Synod report on chaplaincy in 2015 described the role as a 'privilege to be accepted and a call to listen to the stories of those they meet, care for, work with and live alongside every day. Chaplains are allowed to enter into the story and to become part of that story.'[6]

The chaplain's role is therefore primarily one of pastoral care (sharing the love of God), but it also includes elements of mission (sharing the good news) and the prophetic (inspiring change in an institution). I believe this is best summed up as promoting well-being. To illustrate this, I have listed below the tasks of workplace chaplaincy identified by the Industrial Mission Association and highlighted in italics how many tasks seek well-being, through taking people seriously and developing a regular and sustained partnership.[7]

- As a minister of the Christian church a workplace chaplain is *interested in the well-being and prosperity* of individuals, the company, the organization and wider community.
- A chaplain *takes seriously the needs of all* and is here to serve those whose busy working lives are spent serving others.
- A chaplain is committed to visiting on a *regular and sustained basis.* They can set aside *time to listen* to people at all levels of the workplace, small and large.
- A chaplain is *independent, confidential and impartial,* keen to encourage and *help find solutions.*
- A chaplain is here for *people of all faiths and none,* just as the Christian church is for all people.
- A chaplain is concerned about the wider world and the *global connections with the local economy.*
- A chaplain may *raise concerns and issues* and challenge where necessary.
- A chaplain is an ecumenical *representative of the church* in all its denominations, not only a single local congregation.

In the past, there was a conscious divide between parish-based clergy and those involved in workplace chaplaincy.[8] There was a feeling amongst those in chaplaincy that parish-based ministry was an outdated institution, tied up with maintenance of buildings and entrenched congregations rather than being engaged in the secular world, while those in parish-based ministry saw chaplaincy as either an easy option, with its narrow focus on pastoral listening, or as a compromised institution too closely allied to the secular world.

This is changing with the growth in the number of lay chaplains, and an increased breadth of work within chaplaincy. In Derby, for instance, we have over a hundred chaplains working across a wide range of sectors including retail, industry, leisure, emergency services, care homes and public services. These chaplains have developed some very creative thinking on how parishes can use chaplaincy to integrate pastoral care, witness and evangelism.

I want to explore a short case study on how chaplaincy created a sense of well-being, in partnership with the city housing provider on a largely social-housing estate in Derby.

Case Study: Grieve Inn

This was a project initiated by a small missional hub community set up by the Rev'd Darren Howie, a curate at St Peter's Derby based in the Stockbrook estate—a socially deprived area with a higher than average level of crime and addiction. There are also many displaced groups and families from different cultural backgrounds. All this led to isolation, fragmentation and disconnection.

The missional hub community spent some time in spiritual discernment walking the streets and listening to people, the underlying theology being that Jesus comes alongside individuals and communities and meets them where they are at. Christ through us listens and hears, and speaks to the heart of people's issues. Through informal listening and pastoral care on the streets, the café and pubs, the missional hub community began to identify two key issues in the area: first, a lack of gathering spaces on the estate; and secondly, a strong sense of loneliness and disconnectedness in the area.

The Grieve Inn was therefore set up in partnership with Derby Homes, who offered use of one of their community rooms. Its primary aim was to help those who had suffered any form of loss such as: bereavement; divorce; redundancy; poor health etc. It has created a safe space of acceptance, without judgment or a preset agenda. Within this safe space people are given time to share their experience and to listen to others describing aspects of their lives in which there had been times of great vulnerability, shame and fear.

Using a chaplaincy model, the group leaders primarily wanted to be seen simply as human beings rather than experts who had the answers, and were just wounded healers (as Jesus was). Yet, because the Grieve Inn also offers an arena for honesty, it enabled people to express what they thought about God, asking questions like, 'Where was God when we suffered?' or 'Why doesn't God do more to put things right in the world?' Non-judgmental listening and a care for people's well-being meant there were no taboos about what could be said and discussed. The chaplaincy model had begun to move towards a safe community—even church.

What is interesting from this case study is how it began from a place of prayer and spiritual discernment, which in turn led to a chaplaincy-led initiative, working with a social housing provider and offering pastoral care to local people. Yet the end result was the formation of a small community, which began to look remarkably similar to church.[9]

A Church that Seeks to Transform Lives—The Role of Church-led Community Development

Reflecting back on my own story, I see that I spent a lot of time working with partners to serve the needs of the community, for example, the work with FareShare to tackle food hunger. This is community development. The purpose of community development is to come alongside local people and to help bring change not only in their own lives, but also to have an impact on the wider neighbourhood.

In Ward End, I was privileged to work alongside a skilled community development worker. Like chaplains, these workers operate at the interface of the church and the wider community. 'Put simply, community work seeks to facilitate…a level of awareness and cooperation so that people as a group can act together in such a way as to improve their common life.'[10]

Plant argues this is a two-stage process but each stage is inextricably linked: 'In the first instance, it is to develop the quality of community, in order to enhance the lives of the individuals; and second, to assist the self-development of the individual, so that each may better contribute to the work of the community.'[11]

There is, of course, a challenge behind this approach to community development, for ensuring the flourishing of all members of the community also means enabling a diversity of opinions. This inevitably leads to conflict as well as opportunities for collaboration. This creates another role for the community development worker, which is to hold the tension between the individual and collective freedoms of the people they are working with. Therefore 'A crucial role of the community development worker is creating space for critical dialogue.'[12] This is where I have discovered the value of asset-based community development, which focuses initially on the assets—the gifts, skills and abilities present in the community—and not on its needs. This way we are able to empower all individuals to contribute rather than compete as to who has the highest need.

I began to ponder how a Christian approach to community development may differ to that promoted by the state or another voluntary sector organization. I think there are two ways: first, Christians clearly believe that in addition to their empowerment role, community development workers should care for the spiritual welfare of the people involved.

Church-based community workers are well placed to challenge those in positions of power

Secondly, the incarnational approach of the church, combined with the fact they are not employed to speak on behalf of the council, means that church-based community workers are often well placed to challenge those in positions of power. I see church-based community development workers acting with a prophetic voice and offering an impartial view on matters.

To help illustrate these points, I want to turn to my second case study, where a community debt advisor worked in partnership with a local church leading to empowerment not just for individuals but the forming of a new community.

Case Study: Gathering Place

The Gathering Place café is a partnership between St Augustine's Church and Derby City Mission based in Normanton, Derby. This is a highly multicultural area, with numerous cultural and religious groups. As an area it also suffers from low levels of income and employment. This means that many people are dependent on benefits.

St Augustine's had been running a drop-in café for a number of years, but numbers were falling. By partnering with Derby City Mission Jubilee Project, who give advice on issues surrounding debt and benefits, the café was given a new sense of purpose and numbers have risen markedly. Food parcels are given to those who need one, but only following an appointment with a debt adviser. This means the community debt advisor is able to help with issues like budgeting. At the same time the advisor will act as an advocate as they will speak to the council, benefits agency and job centre on people's behalf.

The main feedback from people who attend the Gathering Place is about the holistic nature of the café. Not only are people's physical and financial needs being addressed, but there is also emotional and friendship support, as well as spiritual input. This has led to a strong sense of community at the café, and the emergence of peer support. This means that though some guests attend purely for debt advice, many others continue to attend on a social basis. Over time, a significant number of regulars have emerged who attend most weeks.

For instance, one lady whom I will call *Louise* began to attend the café when both she and her husband had been signed off work with health issues. This had begun a downward spiral into debt. Working with the debt advisor, they were able to get on top of their financial issues. At the same time, they had begun to connect with the people in the café and the husband found it a significant high point in their week. They became regulars at the café and would often be a catalyst for conversations around the tables. Over time *Louise* became interested in the Christian faith and attended church. She continues to attend the café and has become a team member.

This spiritual dimension to the Gathering Place is increasingly important. A prayer book and prayer tree are available, and the café begins with simple morning prayer. It is often just the team that meet to pray, but others join us from time to time. Recently the curate, the Rev'd Sarah Watson, has introduced a monthly Holy Communion. This is a simple service, but Sarah has found that having something tangible seems to be the best way for guests to engage with something spiritual. She shares that 'There have been some really profound moments as we have shared bread and wine, which have been humbling and a privilege.'

This case study shows how a community development approach begins with advocacy for individuals and then together they begin to form a safe community. This in turn leads to self-development for all the individuals such as *Louise*. This creates a mutual building up for the common good. The addition of the spiritual dimension, through the sharing of Holy Communion, shows a holistic care that is able to support people practically, mentally and spiritually, leading to a fuller expression of the Christian gospel expressed in community. Once again, the result is beginning to look a lot like church.

A Church That Seeks to Recognize God is at Work—The Role of Pioneer Ministry

Reflecting back on my own story, I felt I had unexpectedly become a pioneer as a group of people had begun to gather around the community development initiative at St Thomas. I recall being challenged by a colleague, the Rev'd Patrick Douglas, to ensure I was rebuilding church as people, and not just a church building project. He helped me to begin to seek where God was at work in our neighbourhood, and not just in the church-based group.

This is the role of pioneer ministers. They take risks and seek to discern where God is at work beyond the church, pointing to signs of his kingdom in the world. Their starting point, like the chaplain and church-based community development worker, is always to build relationships. However, in the case of a pioneer, there is an intentional approach to prayerfully considering where God is at work in a local community. It is often said that a pioneer needs to spend the first six months to a year simply listening to people and praying. It is important not to be too quick to offer advice or to set up a project.

The emphasis in pioneer ministry is often based on seeking the people of peace in the neighbourhood, places and relationships where there are signs of God's kingdom already at work. In these cases, the church will seek to build partnerships and local networks, rather than establishing their own initiatives. This tends to mean that the type of church that emerges in the medium- to long-term will look very different from traditional church. It is often much simpler and avoids the separation of the sacred and the secular, asking the question, 'Not, what would make people come here? But, what does church look like in this place?'[13]

To help illustrate this approach I want to turn to my third case study, where a pioneer minister spent some time to form a church community, in an area of significant disadvantage in inner-city Derby.

Case Study: Derwent Oak

Derwent Oak is a fresh expression of Christian community. It did not start as a mission project or programme; rather it explicitly sought to form a community. This community would be one that people engaged in rather than simply accepted or received from. This is all due to context.

Derwent is a ward where many organizations have tried to make a lasting impact. Local people—who in some cases are fourth-generation unemployed—feel very vulnerable, and have low self-esteem. Many new initiatives have started there which have raised local expectations, but all too often have led to local disappointment and disengagement.

Derwent is not a place where the church has strong links with the wider community—it has historically been remote, with little reach. Taken together with the local context, it has been important that the church commits to a long process of active listening and building trust, not seeking to rush to solutions or achieving strategic targets and goals.

In 2012, the Rev'd Beth Honey was appointed as a pioneer minister working alongside her husband Ben (who is now also a trained lay pioneer). They have developed a patient and long-term process getting to know their community, and discovering where God is at work in it. Rather than develop projects, they have spent time with people through running events such as community bonfires and BBQs. As they do this, they seek to reveal people's own sense of latent spirituality (to help people see that God might be at work in them). One of their partners working in a 'secular' setting said, *'Derwent Oak's faith is clear and obvious, but never pushed—the wider community know who they are and respect them for it.'*

Derwent Oak is slowly forming a small group that is committed to the local community in loving service and is beginning to work alongside Aspire Wrestling, who focus on working with people with a variety of non-physical conditions—autism, mental health problems, depression, anxiety, learning disabilities etc and using the process of training, working together and performing to positive effect.

Derwent Oak is making links with these people. Creating friendly spaces to eat, together with the time given for prayer, reflection and gentle exploration of Scripture, has resulted in real change in people's lives. These meals often have a sacramental feel about them—the food really matters and is holy to the community. This led in a recent meeting to a community member referring to Derwent Oak as a church. This was the first time that members had been so explicit about who they were!

The pioneering model of ministry being explored and developed at Derwent Oak is based on seeking to be 'authentic, culturally and contextually sensitive...[leading] to an expression of church that is formed for the benefit of those who have never attended church.'[14] It has meant taking a risk and seeking to do something different with people. This more entrepreneurial approach allows considerable freedom to form church around individuals rather than a set model of church imposed by a prayer book. Interestingly, as with chaplaincy and community development, the end result is an emerging Christian community that looks like—but at the same time is very different from—church.

4

The Jews' Story

The previous chapters identified three distinct models of urban mission and how they shaped my ministry and those of my colleagues:

- To seek well-being—this is the role of the chaplaincy;
- To transform lives—this is connected to the role of church-led community development;
- To recognize where God is at work—this is related to the role of pioneer ministry.

I want to turn now to look at the Bible and theology to help us reflect on these different models of urban mission. The biblical lens I want us to reflect through is the Jewish exile. Before the exile the Jewish people lived in a place where they were secure, where everything was ordered and the role of their faith was clear. But exile led to significant change for the Jewish people. 'The things they had been most certain about were called into question. The things that had given them a distinctive identity were destroyed.'[15]

Yet in the midst of this change, the Jews found a new hope and purpose that gave birth to a new form of Judaism, and a significant programme of social and religious reform. They moved away from a national religion based on attending the temple festivals, to smaller community gatherings based around the synagogue. The Jewish faith as we know it emerged. This had an important impact on the way they expressed their faith, how the faith was put into action and on the role of the faith leaders.

The church is facing similar questions to the Jewish exiles, leading to reshaping of our mission

Could this period of transition in the Jewish faith have anything to say to the church today? I feel that as the church enters a post-Christendom era, and the challenges of a multicultural city, the church is facing similar questions to the Jewish exiles, and this is leading to some painful reflection on our faith and some reshaping of our mission. Authors such as Brueggemann, Yoder and Hauerwas have mined the deep resources of 'exilic theology that promises to offer a provocative, creative and helpful set of ideas that modern Christians can derive from the ancient Hebrews and reflect on in their experience.'[16]

To help us in this task, I want to particularly focus on what I call the 'Jeremiah vision' as outlined in Jeremiah's letter to the exiles (Jeremiah 29). In verse 7 God through Jeremiah calls the Jews to 'seek the *shalom* of the city where I have sent you into exile.' This is what I call the Jeremiah vision as it covers three distinct commands given to the exiles:

- First is a call to seek *shalom.*
- The second is a call to engage with the city.
- Finally, a call to recognize God at work.

The Call to Work for Shalom

Jeremiah's first call to the exiles was to seek the *shalom*. This word has a wide range of meaning. Moltmann defines it as 'the blessed joy of a successful life; the fullness of life in mutual love with God; the fullness of life in community; and it is impossible to distinguish between salvation and well-being.'[17]

I find synergies between the call to seek *shalom* and the chaplain's call to seek well-being, physically, psychologically and spiritually. But Jeremiah adds a deeper meaning beyond this definition of flourishing: Jeremiah says that their personal *shalom* was linked to the well-being of the city, 'For it is in working for the city's welfare they will find their welfare' (Jer 29.7). The definition of *shalom* is therefore widened to look not just at their own peace and welfare, but also to share God's grace, healing and salvation.

So, we see that seeking *shalom* takes on a missionary dimension as the Jews are called to bless those around them, as their sense of *shalom* is intrinsically linked with the *shalom* of others. As Murray argues, 'To seek the *shalom* of the city will only happen if one identifies itself with the needs, concerns and aspirations of local people.'[18]

I believe this call to seek *shalom* speaks into the changing role of the church today. Through chaplaincy, our acts of pastoral care can spread beyond the church congregation to other members of our society. This was the position taken by the Church of England in a report to General Synod in 2002.[19]

Although now dated, this report contains a helpful annex outlining some theological principles that are listed below. Once again I have highlighted in italics the synergies with a potential role for the church in seeking *shalom*.

- *The parish system gives the Church of England its distinctive interface.*

- The church's presence in a locality is a prophetic sign of a commitment by people of faith *not to their own betterment but to mutual struggle.*
- Our faith is concerned with welfare of people.
- It is *life giving and life-enhancing.*
- *Our faith is active in engaging and sustaining a hope.*
- Based on a belief that transformation is possible and *offers a different future* where things can be different.
- Our faith sees no distinction between love of God and love of neighbour.
- Rather it offers the possibility that one encounters God in acts of *compassion and solidarity* with the poor.
- We believe that partnership is a vital sign of a common humanity.
- In acting in partnership, we expect a respectful relationship, investment of time and *commitment to empower* and not to exploit.

The Call to Engage with the City

We cannot underestimate the significance of this call to seek *shalom* of the city, and the challenge it was for Jeremiah's readers. This letter represents a stunning and remarkable shift in Old Testament theology. For one would expect the Jewish exiles to despise their captors, to keep themselves pure from the life of the great imperial city.

Yet, Jeremiah's command is to pray for *shalom of the city*. This echoes Psalm 122 when the psalmist prays for the peace of Jerusalem saying, 'May they prosper who love you, peace be within your walls, and security within your towers.' Jeremiah is asking them to pray exactly the same prayer for prosperity, peace and security, but this time the prayer is for their Babylonian oppressors. What a turnaround! Jeremiah is undermining the established view that their peace lay in Jerusalem—and applying it to the evil city of Babylon.

There is little doubt that the dichotomy between Babylon and Jerusalem has influenced theological thinking about the nature of cities. These biblical metaphors have spilled over into popular understanding: 'Babylon has become equated with decadence, sexual immorality, idolatry, and worldly values—the antithesis of the kingdom of God,'[20] while Jerusalem has 'transmogrified into an ideal form—a glimpse of the eternal order, a visible heaven on earth, a seat of life abundant—in other words a utopia.'[21]

With this in mind, we see just how radical the Jeremiah vision is. It undermines the old order that says you only look after your own. Instead, we are called to pray for the healing and salvation of a broken world. It is not just about securing one's own sense of well-being and helping a few others along the way. We connect with the vision of community development, as it is all about rolling one's sleeves up and looking to transform the whole city with all its vices into a better place for everyone.

If we read on in Jeremiah's letter, we see that he does not just give lofty advice; he is immensely practical in his instructions on how to work for God in the city. He calls on the Jews to understand the city's needs as a need to build houses, work the land and provide a better life for their families. We see that God is in the business of community transformation.

The Call to Recognize God at Work

One of the challenges facing the Jews in exile was trying to understand where God was in their predicament. The destruction of the temple, knocking down the walls of the city and deportation of God's chosen king would have deeply affected their faith, especially as their religious identity was so bound up with the national focus on Jerusalem and the duties of temple worship.

Many may have seen the destruction of the temple as the triumph of the Babylonian god Marduk over Yahweh, and therefore the temptation would be to capitulate to the Babylonian theology, allowing its ideas to change their own theology. Furthermore, when they arrived in Babylon, they would have been introduced to all the excesses of Babylonian society, so some may also have been tempted to adopt Babylonian practices and become ensnared by the culture of prosperity. The final temptation may have been to become so inward looking and preoccupied with their survival that they ignored the wider community around them.

The exiles were encouraged to embrace the exile as an act of the will of God

The Jeremiah vision in Jeremiah 29 offered the Jewish exiles another, more radical alternative. They were called to 'view the exile not as a terrible catastrophe but as a God-given chance for a new beginning.'[22] In the oft-quoted verse 11, God gives them a vision of hope and a future—that they are part of something bigger than any chasm of despair they have fallen down. All this is because, as the opening words of the letter make clear, their predicament is an act of God, not the Babylonian king: 'Thus says the Lord of Hosts, the God of Israel, to all the exiles that I have sent into exile from Jerusalem to Babylon.'

This phrase, 'that I have sent into exile,' is one word in the Hebrew—*galah,* and the majority of the biblical occurrences of the word *galah* are in the work of the prophets and the apocalyptic literature and occurrences 'where God is revealed as the one who defines the course of history.'[23] In other words, the exiles were encouraged to embrace the exile as judgment and an act of the will of God. God had not been defeated. They were not at the mercy of circumstances. God himself is revealed as being present amongst the changes.

Just as Jeremiah points to God as the prime mover behind the Jewish sojourn in exile, I see a clear link to the work of a pioneer minister in seeking to recognize how God is at work in our neighbourhoods—looking for the places and relationships where God is at work. The traditional church model is not working because it has tended to focus on maintaining the needs of the *existing* congregations. Just as the recognition of God's presence generated a counter-narrative to the story of the exile, the pioneer's call is to recognize where God is at work, to join in his mission and, through worship, humbly share God's hopes for the future.

Integrating Mission in a Synagogue

The Bible does not tell us how the Jews fulfilled the Jeremiah vision. We get some hints in stories like Daniel, which draws heavily on Jeremiah's letter in recognizing the prophecy of a seventy-year exile. I see clear resonance in the way Daniel and his companions actively seek the transformation of the city of Babylon and recognize God at work in their midst.

But what about the ordinary Jews? How did they respond to the Jeremiah vision? Some historians believe the *synagogues* originated during the Babylonian exile.[24] This is a plausible and attractive suggestion; however, there is no substantiated archaeological evidence. All we know is that the word *synagogue* literally means a meeting or gathering place and that, as such, the *synagogue* was probably an amalgamation of three separate earlier institutions: a prayer house, a study hall or school, and a community centre.[25]

There is a real connection between the three roles of the synagogue and the Jeremiah vision

These new expressions of the Jewish faith were very different from the cultic religion which had led to a religion focused on the temple and priests leading worship. I see a real connection between the three roles of *synagogue* and the Jeremiah vision. The call to pray for the *shalom* of the city would necessitate a gathering to pray; the call to serve the community links to the role of the *synagogue* as a centre for the Jews' social and charity work; while the focus on seeking to recognize where God is at work links to the focus on study and the deuteronomists' desire to learn from their history.

As I noted in earlier chapters, the work of the chaplains, community development workers and pioneers often seems to create a form of new community. Can the church learn from early synagogues? Were these early fresh expressions of the Jewish faith? Could the Jeremiah vision offer a more integrated model of local community gatherings focused on building community through prayer, study, dispensing charity and sharing community meals?

A Future Story?

5

The previous chapters identified three models of urban mission:

- Offering *shalom* through chaplaincy;
- Creating community transformation through community development;
- Pointing to God's presence through pioneering.

What is noticeable, though, is that in all three of the case studies there has been an increasing merging of these approaches—so that the three ministries overlap. This is not surprising as the commands are all integrated in one verse in Scripture and I have artificially broken down the verse into three parts. Furthermore, as I have highlighted above, the commands probably also all began to take expression in the early forms of synagogue during the Jewish exile.

Having said this, many dioceses and denominations continue to train and equip people for these three models of mission in isolation. We see chaplaincy led by a chaplain general, and often led by an ecumenical charity. Community development is led by social responsibility officers (often renamed as community action or community transformation officers), with a myriad of often lay-led project leaders. Finally, pioneers are now selected in a parallel stream to other priests and trained on pioneer courses, co-ordinated by a diocesan missioner or fresh expressions advisor.

This disconnect has led to silo thinking and a lack of joined-up thinking at diocesan or national level. However, on the ground, we see constant overlap between these different ministries. It is my belief that we need to bring these ministries together intentionally. As my earlier case studies showed, by working collectively we can facilitate a holistic engagement with some of our toughest inner-city neighbourhoods.

In line with the scriptural pattern, I would also go further to suggest that the greatest impact is created when we integrate these three mission models in what I call intentional Christian communities. Following the traditions of the synagogues and monastic orders, these intentional Christian communities focus on working for *shalom*, facilitating community transformation and seeking where God is at work and joining in.

To illustrate this proposition, I want to return to my own story and the vision for the St Thomas' Community—the church I now lead—whose origins were described in chapter two.

St Thomas' Community is a small group of individuals who have committed themselves to seeking God's purpose for Pear Tree, Normanton and Rose Hill and seek to express this through a corporate approach to prayer, hospitality and mission.

Prayer for People's Well-being

St Thomas' Community was born in a prayer meeting and there remains a real focus on prayer. As a community, we are committed to praying for the area's well-being. We pray every day: for one another, for the mission of the community and needs of the area. Furthermore, as we have gone out into the streets and parks around St Thomas', we have been both prayer walking and held pop-up events where we have asked for our neighbours' prayer needs and offered to pray for them as opportunities arise.

It is noticeable that each time the doors of St Thomas' are open, people come in and are overwhelmed not only by the building's architectural beauty but also increasingly by a sense of peace and a prayerful presence, and so they will often go on to light a candle and say a prayer themselves.

We are Working to Transform Our Community

George Lings in his research into fresh expressions of church in the Church of England identified a number of community development plants. Making up 20% of all new church plants, he suggests community development plants are based on these principles:

- They are separate enough from institutional church not to be impossibly tarnished by it.
- They are underpinned by Christian values while being engaged in social transformation.
- They have learnt that Christlike actions come before words and concepts.
- They wait to see where God is at work in individuals and respond to opportunities.
- They work within the existing culture rather than taking converts out of the culture.

At St Thomas' Community we are keen to explore how we can adopt this model of faithful presence and continue to find new ways to work with partners to serve the needs in the community of Pear Tree and Rose Hill. Ideas include working with social services to support lonely and isolated people and working with local charities providing for hungry children in school holidays.

Looking for Signs of God at Work

The St Thomas' Community is committed to seeing what God is doing and joining in. So, through both hospitality and engaging with the community where they are, we are working with partners in the locality to explore how St Thomas' Community can come alongside the community and empower them to do the things they are called to do.

It has been good to meet local people and share our stories over a cup of tea, a cake or a more substantial meal. Our logo gives a hint of the direction we are heading—inspired by Ezekiel 47 and Revelation 22, it depicts the river of life that flows out of the temple and into the street where trees grow with 'leaves for the healing of the nations.'

Plans for Reshaping St Thomas' Building—A New Kind of Church

Reflecting on the DNA of the St Thomas' Community, we see parallels with the synagogue and new monastic tradition. This includes a strong focus on intentional community, patterns of prayer, hospitality and practical engagement in mission beyond itself (often to the poor). What holds this new kind of church together? It is not sitting in rows at a Sunday service but following the traditions of the friars—a rhythm of life. This is a commitment to prayer, to meeting one another and to mission—all underpinned by a set of values.

As more and more people catch this vision, I see tangible links with the ancient synagogues and monastic communities. Like them, we are looking to create a shared space for hospitality, a safe space to help meet people at their point of need and a sacred space where we hope to start and end the day in prayer and share a meal together. Like the other case studies in this booklet, we are creating a sense of community together and beginning to form church together.

We are now working with an architect to translate these ideas and values into physical spaces and seeking further funding to create a sustainable long-term vision for St Thomas'. Our initial ideas are to create:

A Shared Space—Where We Build Shalom—Creating Bridges Not Barriers

- Meeting spaces where people can gather in large or small numbers to share together, experience cultural events and learn together, and where schools can visit to appreciate the heritage.
- Breakout spaces for small group training, and a space to offer advice and support.

A Safe Space—Where We Work in Community Development—Offering Hope for Change

- A café space to welcome people as they come into church—where the St Thomas' Community can host conversations, but also look outside the doors to engage with the community.
- The opportunity for several organizations committed to co-locate at St Thomas'to reach out to the community in Pear Tree and Rose Hill. Through potentially creating offices and a hot-desking suite on a first floor we hope to generate shared space to facilitate joint working.

A Sacred Space—Where We Recognize the Image of God in Everyone and Pioneer a New Church

- A dedicated prayer space in the lady chapel that enables daily prayer throughout the day and a space to bring people together at lunchtime to share a meal and maybe Holy Communion.

We will look to retain the chancel as sanctified and keep its heritage open to the large meeting space as a focus for worship on a Sunday.

I do not think I have come to the end of my reflection, but I do see St Thomas' Community as a model of integrated urban mission that brings together the ministries of chaplaincy, community development and pioneer ministry. Following the traditions of the early synagogues and the later monasteries, we are doing this in intentional Christian community, seeking to develop the different skills across the community. At the same time, by developing a common rhythm of life and shared space at the church, we are able to offer a range of ministries intentionally and bring people together for the sake of the gospel.

Notes

1 C Rees, 'Back To The Future: That's Where The Church of England Must Dare To Go,' *The Guardian*, 12 July 2018.

2 Archbishop's Commission On UPAs, *Faith In The City* (London: Church House Publishing, 1985).

3 Working agreement between incumbent and curate, January 2006.

4 Role description for community minister post, March 2011.

5 C Ross, 'The Theology of Partnership,' *IBMR* Vol 34, No 3, July 2010, pp 145–150.

6 General Synod, *Report from the Archbishops' Evangelism Task Group* (London: General Synod of the Church of England, 2015) p 19.

7 IMA, *Faith Economy Work* (Unpublished Study Pack, 2007).

8 G Legood, *Chaplaincy: The Church's Sector Ministries* (London: Cassells, 1999).

9 Sadly the Grieve Inn no longer runs as a group.

10 P Ballard and L Husselbee, *Community and Ministry* (London: SPCK, 2007) p 6.

11 Cited by P Ballard and L Husselbee, *ibid,* p 17.

12 C Packham, *Active Citizenship and Community Learning* (Exeter: Learning Matters, 2008) p 145.

13 A Shier-Jones, *Pioneer Ministry and Fresh Expressions of Church* (London: SPCK, 2009) p 33.

14 *ibid,* pp 6–7.

15 J Holdsworth, *Dwelling in a Strange Land* (Norwich: Canterbury Press, 2003) p 4.

16 D Smith-Christopher, *A Biblical Theology of the Exile* (Minneapolis, MN: Fortress Press, 2002) p 6.

17 J Moltmann, 'Peace, The Fruit Of Justice' p 150 in J Moltmann and J Metz, *Faith and the Future* (London: SCM Press, 1995) pp 147–158.

18 S, Murrray, *City Vision* (London: Daybreak, 1990) p 85.

19 Urban Bishops' Panel, *The Urban Renaissance and the Church of England* (London: General Synod Of Church Of England, 2002).

20 D Watson, 'Babylon In The New Testament' in *Anchor Bible Dictionary* (New York: Doubleday, 1992) p 566.

21 L Mumford, 'Utopia, The City And The Machine,' p 281, *Daedalus* 94, 1965, pp 271–292.

22 R Albertz, *Israel In Exile: The History and Literature of the Sixth Century BCE* (Atlanta, GA: Society of Biblical Literature, 2003) p 7.

23 H-J Zobel, 'Galah' pp 476–488 in *Theological Dictionary of the Old Testament* vol II (Grand Rapids, MI: Eerdmans, 1975) p 487.

24 J Bright, *A History of Israel* (Oxford: Blackwell, third ed, 1981) p 323.

25 S Cohen, 'The Temple and the Synagogue,' pp 151–174 in Truman G Madsen (ed), *The Temple in Antiquity: Ancient Records and Modern Perspectives* (Provo, UT: Religious Studies Center, Brigham Young University, 1984).